THIS GREAT UNKNOWING

BOOKS BY DENISE LEVERTOV

Poetry
The Double Image
Here and Now
Overland to the Islands
With Eyes at the Back of Our Heads
The Jacob's Ladder
O Taste and See
The Sorrow Dance
Relearning the Alphabet
To Stay Alive
Footprints
The Freeing of the Dust
Life in the Forest
Collected Earlier Poems 1940–1960
Candles in Babylon
Poems 1960–1967
Oblique Prayers
Poems 1968–1972
Breathing the Water
A Door in the Hive
Evening Train
Sands of the Well
The Life Around Us
The Stream and the Sapphire
This Great Unknowing: Last Poems

Prose
New & Selected Essays
Tesserae: Memories & Suppositions
The Letters of Denise Levertov & William Carlos Williams

Translations
Guillevic/Selected Poems
Joubert/Black Iris (Copper Canyon Press)

THIS GREAT UNKNOWING
Last Poems

Denise Levertov

With a Note on the Text by Paul A. Lacey

A New Directions Book

Book and cover design by Erik Rieselbach
Manufactured in the United States of America
New Directions Books are printed on acid-free paper
First published clothbound in 1999
First published as New Directions Paperbook 910 in 2000
Published simultaneously in Canada by Penguin Books Canada Limited

PUBLISHER'S NOTE: New Directions owes special thanks for help with
This Great Unknowing to Nikolai Goodman, Paul A. Lacey, Marlene Muller,
and Valerie Trueblood Rapport.

LIBRARY OF CONGRESS CATALOGING-IN-PUBLICATION DATA

Denise Levertov, 1923–1997
This great unknowing: last poems / Denise Levertov;
    with an afterword by Paul A. Lacey.
    p.   cm.
ISBN 0-8112-1403-6 (alk. paper)
ISBN 0-8112-1458-2 (paperbook)
    I. Title
PS3562.E8876T47   1999
811'.54–dc21   98-51469
CIP

New Directions Books are published for James Laughlin
by New Directions Publishing Corporation
80 Eighth Avenue, New York 10011

CONTENTS

THIS GREAT UNKNOWING

FROM BELOW

I move among the ankles
of forest Elders, tread
their moist rugs of moss,
duff of their soft brown carpets.
Far above, their arms are held
open wide to each other, or waving—

what they know, what
perplexities and wisdoms they exchange,
unknown to me as were the thoughts
of grownups when in infancy I wandered
into a roofed clearing amidst
human feet and legs and the massive
carved legs of the table,

the minds of people, the minds of trees
equally remote, my attention then
filled with sensations, my attention now
caught by leaf and bark at eye level
and by thoughts of my own, but sometimes
drawn to upgazing—up and up: to wonder
about what rises
so far above me into the light.

FOR THE ASKING

'You would not seek Me if you did not already possess Me.'

— Pascal

Augustine said his soul
was a house so cramped
God could barely squeeze in.
Knock down the mean partitions,
he prayed, so You may enter!
Raise the oppressive ceilings!
                           Augustine's soul
didn't become a mansion large enough
to welcome, along with God, the women he'd loved,
except for his mother (though one, perhaps,
his son's mother, did remain to inhabit
a small dark room). God, therefore,
would never have felt
fully at home as his guest.
                           Nevertheless,

it's clear desire
fulfilled itself in the asking, revealing prayer's
dynamic action, that scoops out channels
like water on stone, or builds like layers
of grainy sediment steadily
forming sandstone. The walls, with each thought,
each feeling, each word he set down,
expanded, unnoticed; the roof
rose, and a skylight opened.

CELEBRATION

Brilliant, this day—a young virtuoso of a day.
Morning shadows cut by sharpest scissors,
deft hands. And every prodigy of green—
whether it's ferns or lichen or needles
or impatient points of bud on spindly bushes—
greener than ever before.
                              And the way the conifers
hold new cones to the light for blessing,
a festive rite, and sing the oceanic chant the wind
transcribes for them!
A day that shines in the cold
like a first-prize brass band swinging along the street
of a coal-dusty village, wholly at odds
with the claims of reasonable gloom.

PATIENCE

What patience a landscape has, like an old horse,
head down in its field.
                              Grey days,
air and fine rain cling, become one, hovering till at last,
languidly, rain relinquishes that embrace, consents
to fall. What patience a hill, a plain,
a band of woodland holding still, have, and the slow falling
of grey rain ... Is it blind faith? Is it
merely a way to deeply rest? Is the horse
only resigned, or has it
some desireable knowledge, an enclosed meadow
quite other than its sodden field,
which patience is the key to? Has it already,
within itself, entered that sunwarmed shelter?

ANCIENT STAIRWAY

Footsteps like water hollow
the broad curves of stone
ascending, descending
century by century.
Who can say if the last
to climb these stairs
will be journeying
downward or upward?

FIRST LOVE

It was a flower.

There had been,
before I could even speak,
another infant, girl or boy unknown,
who drew me—I had
an obscure desire to become
connected in some way to this other,
even to *be* what I faltered after, falling
to hands and knees, crawling
a foot or two, clambering
up to follow further until
arms swooped down to bear me away.
But that one left no face, had exchanged
no gaze with me.

This flower:
                suddenly
there was *Before I saw* it, the vague
past, and *Now*. Forever. Nearby
was the sandy sweep of the Roman Road,
and where we sat the grass
was thin. From a bare patch
of that poor soil, solitary,
sprang the flower, face upturned,
looking completely, openly
into my eyes.
                I was barely
old enough to ask and repeat its name.

'Convolvulus,' said my mother.
Pale shell-pink, a chalice
no wider across than a silver sixpence.

It looked at me, I looked
back, delight
filled me as if
I, not the flower,
were a flower and were brimful of rain.
And there was endlessness.
Perhaps through a lifetime what I've desired
has always been to return
to that endless giving and receiving, the wholeness
of that attention,
that once-in-a-lifetime
secret communion.

BEYOND THE FIELD

Light, flake by flake touching down on surface tension
of ocean, strolling there before diving forever under.

Tectonic plates inaudibly grinding, shifting—
monumental fidgets.

The mind's far edges twitch, sensing
kinships beyond reach.

Too much unseen, unknown, unknowable,
assumed missing therefore:

shadings, clues, transitions linking
rivers of event, imaged, not imaged, a flood

that rushes towards us, through us, away
beyond us before we wheel to face what seems

a trace of passage, ripple already stilling itself
in tall grass near the fence of the mind's field.

THE MÉTIER OF BLOSSOMING

Fully occupied with growing—that's
the amaryllis. Growing especially
at night: it would take
only a bit more patience than I've got
to sit keeping watch with it till daylight;
the naked eye could register every hour's
increase in height. Like a child against a barn door,
proudly topping each year's achievement,
steadily up
goes each green stem, smooth, matte,
traces of reddish purple at the base, and almost
imperceptible vertical ridges
running the length of them:
Two robust stems from each bulb,
sometimes with sturdy leaves for company,
elegant sweeps of blade with rounded points.
Aloft, the gravid buds, shiny with fullness.

One morning—and so soon!—the first flower
has opened when you wake. Or you catch it poised
in a single, brief
moment of hesitation.
Next day, another,
shy at first like a foal,
even a third, a fourth,
carried triumphantly at the summit
of those strong columns, and each
a Juno, calm in brilliance,

a maiden giantess in modest splendor.
If humans could be
that intensely whole, undistracted, unhurried,
swift from sheer
unswerving impetus! If we could blossom
out of ourselves, giving
nothing imperfect, withholding nothing!

A HUNDRED A DAY

'A million species of plants and animals will be extinct by the turn
of the century, an average of a hundred a day.'
                              —Dr. Mustafa Tolba, Director-General
                              of the U. N. Environment Program

Dear 19th century! Give me refuge
in your unconscious sanctuary for a while,
let me lose myself behind sententious bombazine,
rest in the threadbare brown merino of dowerless girls.
Yes, you had your own horrors, your dirt, disease,
profound injustices; yet the illusion of endless time
to reform, if not themselves, then the world,
gave solace even to gloomy minds. Nature, for you,
was to be marvelled at, praised and conquered,
a handsome heiress; any debate concerned
the origin and subsequent behaviour of species,
not their demise. Virtue, in your heyday
(blessed century, fictive but so real!) was confident
of its own powers. Laxly guarded, your Hesperides
was an ordinary orchard, its fruit
apples of simple hope and happiness.
And though the *ignorant armies*, then as always,
clashed by night, there was
a beckoning future to look to, that bright
Victorian cloud in the eastern sky. The dodo
was pathetic, grotesque in its singular extinction,
its own stupidity surely to blame. It stood alone
on some low hillock of the mind
and was not seen as shocking, nor as omen.

THAT DAY

Across a lake in Switzerland, fifty years ago,
light was jousting with long lances, fencing with broadswords
back and forth among cloudy peaks and foothills.
We watched from a small pavilion, my mother and I,
enthralled.
       And then, behold, a shaft, a column,
a defined body, not of light but of silver rain,
formed and set out from the distant shore, leaving behind
the silent feints and thrusts, and advanced
unswervingly, at a steady pace,
toward us.
       I knew this! I'd seen it! Not the sensation
of déjà vu: it was Blake's inkwash vision,
'The Spirit of God Moving Upon the Face of the Waters'!
The column steadily came on
across the lake toward us; on each side of it,
there was no rain. We rose to our feet, breathless—
and then it reached us, took us
into its veil of silver, wrapped us
in finest weave of wet,
and we laughed for joy, astonished.

ELEPHANT EARS

I've given up wearing earrings.
Like my mother's, my ears are large—
and mine are lopsided. Now, with age,
the lobes show a crease, and seem to droop
like a Buddha's. But Buddhist tradition
links such big ears to wisdom—
should that console me? My big-eared mother,
although not foolish, was not so much wise
as ardent, responsive, eager to learn.
At the age I am now, she still wore her various pairs
of beautiful earrings with confidence,
and they became her. Perhaps that éclat
was her wisdom—for now, and maybe forever,
a wisdom beyond my reach.
Should I call upon Buddha, on Ganesh,
upon that part of my mother
which lives in me, for enlightenment?
For the chutzpa to dangle jewels
from long and uneven lobes?

ANIMAL SPIRITS

When I was five and
undifferentiated energy, animal spirits,
pent-up desire for the unknown built in me
a head of steam I had
no other way to let off, I ran
at top speed back and forth
end to end of the drawingroom,
bay to French window, shouting—
roaring, really—slamming
deliberately into the rosewood
desk at one end, the shaken
window-frames at the other, till the fit
wore out or some grownup stopped me.

But when I was six I found better means:
on its merry gallows
of dark-green wood my swing, new-built,
awaited my pleasure, I rushed
out to it, pulled the seat
all the way back to get a good start, and
vigorously pumped it up to the highest arc:
my legs were oars, I was rowing a boat in air—
and then, then from the furthest
forward swing of the ropes
                    I let go and flew!
At large in the unsustaining air,
flew clear over the lawn across
the breadth of the garden
and fell, Icarian, dazed,

among hollyhocks, snapdragons, love-in-a-mist,
and stood up uninjured, ready
to swing and fly over and over.

The need passed as I grew;
the mind took over, devising
paths for that force in me, and the body curled up,
sedentary, glad to be quiet and read and read,
save once in a while, when it demanded
to leap about or to whirl—or later still
to walk swiftly in wind and rain
long and far and into the dusk,
wanting some absolute, some exhaustion.

THE POODLE PALACE

I never pass the Poodle Palace
with its barber pole in the shape
of a striped beribboned bone and the sign:
Specializing in Large and Matted Dogs,
without remembering the bitter wonder
of the taxi-driver from somewhere in India
who asked me,
'What is that, Poodle Palace?
What does it mean?'—and when I told him,
laughed, and for blocks,
laughed intermittently, a laughter
dry as fissured earth,
angry and sharp as the ineradicable
knowledge of chronic famine,
of human lives given to destitution
from birth to death. A laugh
in which the stench of ordure
simmered, round which a fog of flies
hovered, a laugh laughed to himself,
whether in despair or hatred, and not
as a form of address: he was indifferent
to whether I heard it or not.

SWIFT MONTH

The spirit of each day passes, head down
under the wind, arms folded.
Ambiguous brothers of those envisioned
'daughters of Time,' proffering neither
gifts nor scorn, their hands
grip elbows, hidden in wide sleeves
of shadow-colored caftans. Day after day
and none lagging, the pace of their stride
not hurried, yet swift, too swift.

A NEW FLOWER

Most of the sunflower's bright petals
had fallen, so I stripped the few
poised to go, and found myself
with a new flower: the center,
that round cushion of dark-roast
coffee brown, tipped with uncountable
minute florets of gold, more noticeable
now that the clear, shiny yellow was gone,
and around it a ring of green, the petals
from behind the petals, there all the time,
each having the form of sacred flame
or bo-tree leaf, a playful, jubilant form
(taken for granted in Paisley patterns)
and the light coming through them, so that
where, in double or triple rank, like a bevy
of Renaissance angels, they overlapped,
there was shadow, a darker shade
of the same spring green—a new flower
on this fall day, revealed within
the autumn of its own brief bloom.

A CRYPTIC SIGN

August. The woods are silent.
No sway of treetops, no skitter of squirrels,
no startled bird. Sky fragments
in rifts of canopy,
palest silken blue.
                    In the crook
of an old and tattered snag
something gleams amid the stillness,
drawing the gaze: some bit of heartwood
so long exposed, weather and time
have polished it, as centuries
of awed lips, touching
a hand of stone, rub it
to somber gleaming.

FEET

I

In the forties, wartime London, I read
an ode by Neruda I've never found again,
about celery—celery the peasant, trudging
stony Andean ridges to market on poor
frayed feet.
        I could search out the *Obras Completas*
I know ... But even if I never find it again,
those green fibrous feet, upholding
the tall stooped form with its flimsy cockscomb
of yellowing leaves, plodded
through me as if through the thin
mountain air, maintaining
their steady, painful, necessitous trudge, and left
their prints in my dust.

II

Travestied by Disney, the Mermaid's real story
has gone underground for now, as books do
if they're abused. As Andersen told it, the tale
was not for young children, not even called
'The Little' — just, 'The Mermaid.' It's about love and grief,
a myth of longing and sacrifice, far closer, say,
to Goethe's *Parable* than to any jovial folktale,
much less to today's manufactured juvenile distractions.

The Mer-folk live for three hundred years, then dissolve
in foam of the wave, and forever vanish
into non-being; humans, the mermaid learns, rarely live
for even one hundred years, often far fewer, but they possess
immortal souls, and rise to continue living
in starlit regions merfolk can never see.
                              In her resolve to love and be loved
by the human prince she had rescued once
from storm and shipwreck, and gain for herself
such a soul, the mermaid goes to the terrible
ocean witch, and obtains a potion to turn her golden-scaled
fish-tail into legs and feet —
and gives up her voice in payment. She does this
knowing each gliding, graceful step she will take
will bring her the pain of walking on knives.
She does this for love, and the dream
of human joys and a deathless soul.
                              There's more,
much more to the story — even a kind of
happy ending, after the final sacrifice, a concession

Andersen made to his time and place. But what endures
along with the evocation of undersea gardens,
of moonlight, of icebergs and coral, and of that same yearning
we find in the Silkie tales and in *The Forsaken Merman*,
are the knifeblades under her feet, unguessed-at
by any who see her glide and dance; and the torment
of having no tongue to speak her love, to speak
her longing to earn a soul.
                                        Something in this
made my mother shed tears when she read it aloud,
her voice for a moment baffled—
and this when her closet was still full of elegant shoes
with the pointed toes of fashion. Did she foresee (and forget
till the next reading) the misery
old age and poor circulation and years of those narrow shoes
would bring her? Certainly she had no doubt
of her own soul; no, what hurt her
was the mermaid's feet. Her agony without complaint,
her great love, courage, unfathomed sorrow,
would not have equally moved my mother
without that focussed sense of each step the mermaid took
being unbearable, yet borne, the firm support
we count on torn away, invisibly shredded.

III

I watched a man whose feet were neatly wrapped in green plastic
enter the restaurant that advertised a $2.00 special. Sloppy Joes.
And I saw him immediately come out again. It was cold and wet,
and I was sheltering under the canvas awning till my bus was due.
He stood there too, and I could sense that he was fuming. 'What
happened?' I ventured. He looked at me. Good eyes, I thought. 'No
shoes,' he said.

I know the rule, 'no shoes, no service' is supposed to be in the in-
terests of hygiene, but I've never understood how. Whatever dirt
and germs bare feet bring in, shoes bring too. Why anyone would
want to walk barefoot on filthy sidewalks is another mystery – but
that's a matter of personal choice. In this instance the man was, in
any case, not barefoot: several layers of heavy-duty green garbage-
bag plastic hid his feet and were tied firmly at the ankles. The
arrangement made me think of Russian serfs, birchbark shoes...

'I've got the money,' he said, and showed it me in his hand – two
bucks, and a few pennies for the tax. How *unfair!* He fumed, I
fumed, the rain poured off the awning, a steady curtain. He
looked quite young, under 40. Did I say he was Black? He hadn't
the look of a drunk or a druggy; looked a bit young for a Vietnam
Vet. When I offered to go in and protest to the manager he didn't
like the idea, and I saw he would feel it a humiliation. I shouldn't
have suggested that.

'What happened to your shoes – did they fall apart?' I asked shyly.
'A guy stole them in the night.' I acknowledged, silently, the
naiveté of my own shock at this robbery of one destitute man by

another. He could get some second-hand shoes at Goodwill or the Salvation Army, he told me, but he was hungry, had wanted to eat before the long walk to the missions. I guessed he had spent the night under the freeway. This street where we stood, near the college, was mostly upscale—this 'luncheon special' at a place which referred to itself as an 'Eatery,' was the only thing of its kind. I thought with disgust of Sloppy Joes, trying to imagine being hungry enough to want one.

I offered him the price of a pair of the cheapest shoes you could buy; I'd noticed them in the window of an Outlet store. He accepted with dignity. When I found myself wondering if in fact he would spend the money on shoes, I realized he might do better with good hand-me-downs than cheap new ones. By then the rain let up and we went our ways.

If affluent Whites took it into their heads to wrap their feet in plastic, a new fashion, how long would the 'eateries' exclude them?

IV

Still in her 80s when she first lived there,
    she loved
            to tramp over the *cerro* above the town;
it reminded her
    of Wales and the freedom
            of long girlhood walks in all weathers.
Here as there, the hills and mountains,
    layer beyond layer,
            ranged themselves like advancing breakers,
though they broke on no shore;
    cloud-shadows stroked them, brightness
            flowed in again as the shadows
moved on. But in time
    her strength failed her.
            She walked only down to the town's
mercado to buy the fruit she craved,
    and exchange a word or two
            with the market women,
the vendors of juice or trinkets, and give her letters
    into the hands of sour-faced
            post-office clerks. In the *Zocalo*
she could watch with pleasure the playing children
    or with amusement
            the foolish antics of tourists. Everywhere
the familiar faces of strangers.
    Then, climbing back up the hilly streets,
            ill-paved, high-kerbed, often,
by her mid-80s, she needed to pause,
    to stop and rest in a cool dark church.
            Once, and more than once, perhaps,

her feet pained her so much that weakness
           overcame her,
                    she sat there crying,
desolate in the need to rise and walk on,
           four or five blocks to her room,
                    her bed, her books, her patio—
accidental pilgrim
           in a strange land.
                    When, my next visit,
I'd found her slippers padded and soft
           yet sturdy enough for the *calle*
                    you'd think I'd brought her the moon and stars...

We begin our lives with such small,
           such plump and perfect
                    infant feet, slivers of pink pearl for toenails,
it's laughable to think of their ever sustaining
           the whole weight of a body.
                    And end them sometimes
with gnarled and twisted objects
           in which are inscribed
                    whole histories—wars, and uprootings,
and long
           patient or impatient sufferings,
                    layer beyond layer,
successions of light and shadow, whole ranges.
           But no recollection
                    of what our feet were like
before we put them to work.

V

Certain phrases recur—not main motifs but occasional
mini-cadenzas on flute, curling
brief as foam above stir and onrush of waves.
'Beautiful are the feet of the swallow
folded unseen past the mountain' —
or, 'Blessèd are the feet
of him who brings good tidings.'

Beautiful, too one's own feet if they've stayed
more or less straight and strong through decades,
and one walks for miles by the sea or through fields and woods
or spends a joyful day in a great museum, arriving
at opening time, staying till closing, grateful to be so upheld.

Yet what prevails is harsh. The mermaid's knives.
My mother's tears. Or the shame
an aging poet felt when, bulky in body, diabetic,
she had to call upon someone to cut her toenails, and not just anyone,
someone (small and deft) in whose country we were guests,
a country our own was bombing, defoliating, attempting,
with all its mechanical power,
                              to obliterate.
With exacting care the Vietnamese nurse performed the procedure,
a doctor checked to see all was as close to well as possible,
and Muriel obediently stretched out her long thin legs, submitting,
grateful but deeply embarrassed: these ministrations
were given by those accustomed to dress the wounds
of footless or armless children,

of peasants whose hands were gone. Her feet
felt better, her soul was mortified.

And still those brief cadenzas
recur – 'Blessèd are the feet
of him who brings good tidings,' – 'Beautiful
are the feet of the swallow
folded unseen past the mountain.'

VI

Maundy Thursday. As prearranged, twelve chairs
are placed in a row before the altar, and twelve parishioners
seat themselves, and take off their shoes and clean socks.
As the old priest and the young one bend to their task,
one stiff, one supple, and carry the shining bowls of fresh warm water
to each presented pair of prewashed feet,
and wash them again and dry them on white, white towels,
the humble ritual, so ancient, so much an act of the body,
a sanctification of flesh (even though, at times,
proud prelates and small bigotted men have been the enactors)
stirs the heart, as true theater must, even in an age
with so loose or lost a connection to symbolic power.

But this is a good time to reflect on how dusty,
scarred by worn sandals, dirty between the toes, grime
on the calloused soles, the apostles' feet would have been.
And mind moves on to worse: old winos stumbling along,
unwashed, their long nails thick as horn, shoes wrong-sized, broken.
And not just winos—anyone homeless, who has to keep moving all day
with no place to go, even if shelter at night
gives them a chance to bathe their blisters, must know
week by week an accretion of weariness, once-good shoes
grown thin; must know a mounting sense of frayed and helpless
fiber at the ends of swollen legs, although they have never imagined
the endless foot-after-foot journey of peasant celery.

FUGITIVES

The Red Cross vans, laden with tanks of
drinking water, can go no further:
the road has become a river.
The dry, dusty, potholed road
that was waiting the rainy season
is flowing with men and women
(especially women) and children.
Silent in stumbling haste,
almost all of them. Only the wailing
of young babies, hungry and terrified,
wafts over the lava-flow
that brims and hurries, dividing briefly
to pass the impediment that each van
is to them, impervious to their purpose
(the first one caught in the flood,
the remaining small convoy already attempting
to back, inch by inch, to where, miles behind them,
they might turn).
                    From a plane,
the road—the river—would look
like one of those horrible nature films
about insects moving as one in some
instinctive ritual; horrible because
though one by one each creature might have
some appealing feature, *en masse* they are
inexorable, a repulsive teeming collective ...
But these are people, and the Red Cross driver,
one of the last to remain in what seems
an unhelpable land of terror, knows it,

sees it, feels it. He has not the distant
impersonal gaze of a pilot high overhead watching
an insect swarm. He deeply perceives
war has deprived these humans, his fellows,
of choice of action. Diminished them. And they advance,
dazed, haggard, unstoppable, driven
less by what shreds of hope may cling to their bodies
than by a despair that might well have left them
paralyzed in the dust, inert before imminent slaughter,
but which some reflex, some ancient trigger in brain-tissue,
propels into grim motion thousand upon thousand,
westward to zones Relief has already fled from.

DARK LOOKS

Strange: today the mountain
—circled by curly cherub clouds
beyond the glittering lake
and vague middle-distance—

looks dark, not snowy,
at odds with the benign
October light, a frowning
humorless old prophet,

sullen among the putti.

Memory demands so much,
it wants every fiber
told and retold.
                         It gives and gives
but for a price, making you
risk drudgery, lapse
into document, treacheries
of glaring noon and a slow march.
Leaf never before
seen or envisioned, flying spider
of rose-red autumn, playing
a lone current of undecided wind,
lift me with you, take me
off this ground of memory that clings
to my feet like thick clay,
exacting gratitude for gifts and gifts.
Take me flying before
you vanish, leaf, before
I have time to remember you,
intent instead on being
in the midst of that flight,
of those unforeseeable words.

ROAST POTATOES

Before the Wholesale Produce Market
moved to the Bronx, what wild
Arabian scenes there'd be each night
across from our 5th floor window—
the trucks arriving from all over
as if at a caravanserai under the weird
orange-bright streetlights
(or was it the canvas awnings that were orange,
sheltering the carrots, the actual oranges...)
Great mounds of fruit, mountain ranges
of vegetables spread in the stalls, and now
more unloading, and the retail trucks
rolling up to bargain and buy till dawn...
Unemployed men, casual labor, hung around,
waiting for clean-up jobs; some were glad
to get some bruised produce if no work.
And the Catholic Worker pickup
came by at the last
for anything unsold, unsaleable (but not
uncookable). In the '60s
there was the Bowery, yes, and ordinary
urban winos, but not
throngs of homeless men
and hardly ever a homeless woman except
for those you'd see down at Maryhouse or sometimes
(conspicuous, embarrassing), in the waiting room at Grand Central.
There were men, though, among those frequenting the market,
who clearly had no fixed abode; we thought of them

as old fashioned hobos.
Some time in the night, or weekends
when the big parking lot, the whole
commercial neighborhood (vanished now), was deserted,
they'd build fires in old metal barrels
and sit round them on upturned crates
roasting fallen potatoes they'd salvaged,
(a regular feast once when a truck
lost its load) and talking, telling stories,
passing a bottle if they had one.
The war was (remotely) gearing up,
Vietnam a still unfamiliar name,
the men were down on their luck,
some White, some Black, not noticeably hostile,
most of them probably drunks:
you couldn't call it
a Golden Age; and yet
around those fires, those roasting potatoes,
you could see, even from our top-storey windows,
not even down there catching the smoky
potato-skin smell or hearing
fragments of talk and laughter—*something*
—you name it, if you know, I can't...
something you might call blessèd? Is that hyperbole? Something kind?
Something not to be found in the '90s, anyway.
Something it seems we'll have to enter the next millennium
lacking, and for the young,

unknown to memory.

VISITATION. OVERFLOW.

I

The slender evidence ...

The *you must take*
my word for it.

The intake of a word.
Its taste, cloud in the mouth.

The presence, invisible,
impalpable, air to
outstretched arms,

but voiced, tracked easily
in room's geography,
among the maps, the gazing-window,
door, fire, all in place, internal
space immutable.

The slenderness
of evidence, narrow backed
tapir undulating
away on
rainforest paths, each tapir bearing
a human soul.

2

Amazon basin,
filling, overflowing,
spirits in every
plant, in bark, in every
animal, in
juice of bark. Words taken

by lips, tongue, teeth, throat,
down into body's
caverns, to enter

blood, bone, breath, as here:

as here the presence
next to that window, appearance

known not to sight,
          to touch,
but to hearing, yes, and yet
appearing, apprehended

in form, in color, by
some sense unnamed,

3

moving slenderly
doorwards, assured, re-
assuring, leaving

a trace, of certainty, promise
broader than slender
tapir's disappearing
sturdy back, the
you can only
take my
word for it, a life,
a phase,
beyond the
known geography, beyond familiar

inward, outward,
outward, inward. A

'time and place' (other terms
                    unavailing)
of learning, of casting
off of dross, as when

hunters steam off fur, skin,
feathers in cauldrons, leaving

the flesh to share
with all, the humble
feast, slender

evidence, take it
or leave it, I give you
my word.

The mountain's daily speech is silence.
Profound as the Great Silence
between the last Office and the first.
Uninterrupted as the silence God maintains
throughout the layered centuries.
All the mountain's moods,
frank or evasive,
its whiteness, its blueness,
are shown to sight alone.
Yet it is known
that fire seethes in its depths
and will surely rise one day, breaking open
the mute imperturbable summit. Will the roar of eruption be
the mountain's own repressed voice,
or that of the fire? Does the mountain
harbor a demon distinct from itself?

Scraps of moon

Scraps of moon
bobbing discarded on broken water

but sky-moon
complete, transcending

all violation.

MASS OF THE MOON ECLIPSE

Not more slowly than frayed
human attention can bear, but slow
enough to be stately, deliberate, a ritual
we can't be sure will indeed move
from death into resurrection.
As the bright silver inch by inch
is diminished, options vanish,
life's allurements. The last sliver
lies face down, back hunched, a husk.

But then, obscured, the whole sphere can be seen
to glow from behind its barrier shadow: bronze,
unquenchable, blood-light. And slowly,
more slowly than desolation overcame, overtook
the light, the light
is restored, outspread in a cloudless pasture of
spring darkness where firefly planes
fuss to and fro, and humans
turn off their brief attention
in secret relief. No matter: the rite
contains its power, whether or not
our witness rises toward it;
grandeur plays out the implacable drama
without even flicking aside our trivial
absence, the impatience with which we
fail to respond.
                    And yet

we are spoken to, and sometimes

we do stop, do, do give ourselves leave
to listen, to watch. The moon,
the moon we do after all
love, is dying, are we to live
on in a world without moon? We swallow
a sour terror. Then
that coppery sphere, no-moon become once more
full-moon, visible in absence.
And still without haste, silver
increment by silver
increment, the familiar, desired,
disregarded brilliance
is given again, given and given.

ONCE ONLY

All which, because it was
flame and song and granted us
joy, we thought we'd do, be, revisit,
turns out to have been what it was
that *once*, only; every initiation
did not begin
a series, a build-up: the marvelous
       did happen in our lives, our stories
       are not drab with its absence: but don't
expect now to return for more. Whatever more
there will be will be
unique as those were unique. Try
to acknowledge the next
song in its body-halo of flames as utterly
present, as now or never.

MID-DECEMBER

Westering sun a mist of gold
between solemnities of crowded vertical
poplar twigs. The mountain's
western slope is touched
weightlessly with what will be, soon,
the afterglow.

TRANSLUCENCE

Once I understood (till I forget, at least)
the immediacy of new life, Vita Nuova,
redemption not stuck in linear delays,
I perceived also (for now) the source
of unconscious light in faces
I believe are holy, not quite transparent,
more like the half-opaque whiteness
of Japanese screens or lampshades,
grass or petals imbedded in that paper-thin
substance which is not paper as this is paper,
and which permits the passage of what is luminous
though forms remain unseen behind its protection.
I perceived that in such faces, through
the translucence we see, the light we intuit
is of the already resurrected, each
a Lazarus, but a Lazarus (man or woman)
without the memory of tomb or of any
swaddling bands except perhaps
the comforting ones of their first
infant hours, the warm receiving-blanket...
They know of themselves nothing different
from anyone else. This great unknowing
is part of their holiness. They are always trying
to share out joy as if it were cake or water,
something ordinary, not rare at all.

DRAWN IN AIR

The arc of branch is not perfect.
Before it reaches
conclusion (and the gratuitous
upcurve of terminal twig,
a playful coda), it falters, losing
for a moment the impetus
that arched its outsetting.
This brief hesitation into
straightness; that post-arrival
flourish; and the way,
being a branch, it tapers, even
the arc's upmost passage
more slender than when it left
the main stem: these,
taken together, are what
gives this unremarkable branch
of an aging, tallish, unpruned peartree
its peculiar charm,
the charm of a master's line—
Degas, Holbein, chalk or pencil,
gathering strength and emphasis,
letting it wane, suggesting
contour but offering to the eyes
a pleasure in simply
line as line.

NOBLESSE OBLIGE

With great clarity, great precision, today
the mountain presents not only
all of its height but a keener sense
of breadth. It seems
nearer than usual;
yet it maintains
the lonely grandeur nothing can challenge:
this open approach,
this way of proclaiming that spring
at last is come, this ceremonious
baring of snowy breast as if
its arms were thrown wide, is not
an attempt at intimacy.
                    (Meanwhile,
            the April sun, cold though it is,
            has opened the small daisies,
            so many and so humble they get underfoot—
            and don't care. Each one
            a form of laughter.)
The mountain graciously continues
its measured self-disclosure.

MASQUERADE

Today the mountain,
playful and not omniscient, thinks itself
concealed among
attendant clouds.
                    Their white and blue
            are a perfect match for yours,
            O mountain! But you are no more hidden
            by complacent cumulus
            than Venus by a mask
            of black Venetian velvet.
            Like a *cavaliere*
            astounded, in the piazza's twilight throng,
            to discern her goddess-flesh,
            I recognize
            amidst imponderable white
            wafting billows, your naive force,
            mountain,
            dense, unmoving.

ENDURING LOVE

It was the way
as they climbed the steps
they appeared bit by bit
yet swiftly—
the tops of their hats
then their faces
looking in as they reached
the top step by the door, then
as I flung the door open
their dear corporeal selves,
first him, then her. It was
the simultaneously
swift and gradual advent
of such mercy after
I had been wounded.
It was the little familiar
net attached to her hat,
it was especially
the thick soft cloth of his black
clerical overcoat,
and their short stature
and their complete
comforting embrace,
the long-dead
visiting time from eternity.

IMMERSION

There is anger abroad in the world, a numb thunder,
because of God's silence. But how naive,
to keep wanting words we could speak ourselves,
English, Urdu, Tagalog, the French of Tours,
the French of Haiti...

                      Yes, that was one way omnipotence chose
to address us—Hebrew, Aramaic, or whatever the patriarchs
chose in their turn to call what they heard. Moses
demanded the word, spoken and written. But perfect freedom
assured other ways of speech. God is surely
patiently trying to immerse us in a different language,
events of grace, horrifying scrolls of history
and the unearned retrieval of blessings lost for ever,
the poor grass returning after drought, timid, persistent.
God's abstention is only from human dialects. The holy voice
utters its woe and glory in myriad musics, in signs and portents.
Our own words are for us to speak, a way to ask and to answer.

A CLEARING

What lies at the end of enticing
country driveways, curving
off among trees? Often only
a car graveyard, a house-trailer,
a trashy bungalow. But this one,
for once, brings you
through the shade of its green tunnel
to a paradise of cedars,
of lawns mown but not too closely,
of iris, moss, fern, rivers of stone rounded
by sea or stream,
of a wooden unassertive large-windowed house.
The big trees enclose
an expanse of sky, trees and sky
together protect the clearing.
One is sheltered here
from the assaultive world
as if escaped from it, and yet
once arrived, is given (oneself
and others being a part of that world)
a generous welcome.
                              It's paradise
as a paradigm for how
to live on earth,
how to be private and open
quiet and richly eloquent.
Everything man-made here
was truly made by the hands
of those who live here, of those

who live with what they have made.
It took time, and is growing still
because it's alive.
It is paradise, and paradise
is a kind of poem; it has
a poem's characteristics:
inspiration; starting with the given;
unexpected harmonies; revelations.
It's rare among
the worlds one finds
at the end of enticing driveways.

SOUTHERN CROSS

(After a sculpture by Philip McCracken)

A darkness rivered, swirled, meandered
by fathomless fiery currents.
Dense abyss of planes and angles,
pinned by unblinking constellations,
celestial stigmata.
And at the core,
bright blood of the wounded wood
(not cut, riven
by secret canker
now revealed)
tardily down the rough cleft
descends and beads.

DESCENDING SEQUENCE

'It was a fearful thing
to come into a man's heart...'
                    —William Carlos Williams, "Winter Sunset"

What I thought to be a river
turned out to be sky.
What I thought were shore, island,
rocks, river-mist,
turned out to be cloud, shadow,
shot-holes in sky's canvas.
Even the deepest shade
down near the horizon
turned out not to be earth,
the real horizon was lower still.
At the oblong world's
very base,
further darkness, a round-topped tree,
a telephone pole, the sharp
ridge of a roof, chimney, gable end:
silhouettes on a sky
differently white, not the illusory
river's whiteness—and all
very small under the huge
vista above. Small,
as if in fear.

ALIENATION IN SILICON VALLEY

I'd like to invoke a different world,
a history more past than future, yes,
but present in fragments, hinting itself onward
in here a word or there a grace that's
taken for granted—evoke and hold it.
Ancestral, painful, but mine by right.
But soberly I have to admit
it's only by virtue of being outside those worlds
I can perceive them.
                              What can I make, then,
of this one, inside it
but not at home? 'Here,' de Toqueville said,
(not this far west, but at what was then the edge)
'they live from hand to mouth,
like an army on the march—'
severed from history.
I am told of orchards, clouds of blossom,
crimson peaches, fragrant apricots,
forty years back, fifty at most, where now
a vacuous clutter of buildings fills up
square mile after mile; and I can cast
on my mind's screen an orchard,
acres of orchards—but I never
touched their earth. Nostalgia
comes if it must, but is not for borrowing.
I see, I know, the desecration, I taste
the degrading sickly bile of that knowledge—
but I did not witness flower or fruit,

a specific locus, ancestral ground.
What I hold are the links the mind
forges between a vanished field of imagined trees
and their peers remembered, the shine
of stolen cherries, far off
in time and in place; and also by now perhaps
vanished, that field built over.

MOMENTS OF JOY

A scholar takes a room on the next street,
the better to concentrate on his unending work, his word,
his world. His grown children
feel bereft. He comes and goes while they sleep.
But at times it happens a son or daughter
wakes in the dark and finds him sitting
at the foot of the bed
in the old rocker; sleepless
in his old coat, gazing
into invisible distance, but clearly there to protect
as he had always done.
                    The child springs up and flings
arms about him, presses
a cheek to his temple, taking him by surprise,
and exclaims, 'Abba!' – the old, intimate name
from the days of infancy.
And the old scholar, the father,
is deeply glad to be found.
That's how it is, Lord, sometimes:
You seek, and I find.

THINKING ABOUT PAUL CELAN

Saint Celan,
stretched on the cross
of survival,

pray for us. You
at last could endure
no more. But we

live and live,
blithe in a world
where children kill children.

We shake off
the weight of
our own exemption,

we flourish,
we exceed
our allotted days.

Saint Celan,
pray for us
that we receive

at least a bruise,
blue, blue, unfading,
we who accept survival.

AWARE

When I opened the door
I found the vine leaves
speaking among themselves in abundant
whispers.
        My presence made them
hush their green breath,
embarrassed, the way
humans stand up, buttoning their jackets,
acting as if they were leaving anyway, as if
the conversation had ended
just before you arrived.
                I liked
the glimpse I had, though,
of their obscure
gestures. I liked the sound
of such private voices. Next time
I'll move like cautious sunlight, open
the door by fractions, eavesdrop
peacefully.

A NOTE ON THE TEXT

Had Denise Levertov lived longer, at least two things would be different about this book: it would have contained more poems, and they would have been organized, probably into subsections, according to thematic or other aesthetic principles. And it is more than likely that she would have had a different title than *This Great Unknowing*, the one the editors have chosen from her poem "Translucence," in this volume. This book, however, is neither loosely nor thoughtlessly thrown together; we have deliberately chosen to print the poems as they appear in a loose-leaf book where, according to her last secretary, Marlene Muller, "in general, the poems are numbered from the oldest to the most recent."

*

As one goes on living and working, themes recur, transposed into another key perhaps. Single poems that seemed isolated perceptions when one wrote them prove to have struck the first note of a scale or a melody.... Though the artist as craftsman is making discrete and autonomous works ... the artist as explorer in language of the experiences of his or her life is, willy-nilly, weaving a fabric, building a whole in which each discrete work is a part that functions in some way in relation to all the others.

Denise Levertov described her earliest books of poetry as gatherings of poems rather than compositions. Poems which should "have been in a single book together because of their interrelationships were arbitrarily divided between *Here and Now* and *Overland to the Islands.*" Those two books she said were loosely, thoughtlessly thrown together, "and for the first time I realized that a book of separate poems can in itself be a composition, and that to compose a book is preferable to randomly gathering one."

In all her subsequent books, Denise Levertov carefully arranged the order of poems so that both individual works and groups of poems could throw light on one another and themes and counter-themes could weave larger patterns. From *The Sorrow Dance* on, her common way of "composing" her books was to organize her poems into subsections, often headed by a title, phrase, or image from a poem. When she brought poems together from earlier books and reconstructed patterns to compose *To Stay Alive*, she justified her action on aesthetic grounds—"it assembles separated parts of a whole."

> It happens at times that the poet becomes aware of the relationships that exist between poem and poem; is conscious, after the act, of one poem, one line or stanza, having been the precursor of another.... And then, to get the design clear—'for himself and thereby for others,' Ibsen put it—he must in honesty pick up that thread, bring the cross reference into its rightful place in the inscape, the Gestalt of his life (his work)/his work (his life).

Denise Levertov's habits of composition were very well established. She wrote only in longhand, and she revised for as long as a poem kept her reworking it. When I was working with her papers in 1984, I came across a cache of some twenty-five pages of reworking or simply fiddling with one section of her Notebook poem. Some pages were from writing pads, inscribed on the long side, some were small scraps of paper, backs of envelopes, even an airline seating-stub with a few words on it. I found a number of smaller caches for other poems. Such scrupulous attention to the details of a poem was characteristic. She would hand-copy a poem, incorporating all the revisions, until she had a fair copy, then have it typed. When the clean copy came, she would go over it again and make any further revisions demanded by her aesthetic sense. As long as anything kept her revising, the poem was unfinished. When she could leave a typed copy alone, the poem was done.

She was as meticulous in her readings as she was in her writing. She did not read unfinished poems. She kept two copies of the loose-leaf book of finished poems being gathered for a new book: one copy she took to use at readings; the other never left the house. As individual poems were published in journals, that would be noted in the master book's table of contents. So far as we can tell, then, the order in which the poems were entered into this loose-leaf book was the order in which the poet let them out of her hands, satisfied that they were now complete.

This Great Unknowing is the only book of Denise Levertov's, then, where we can have some confidence that we are seeing how the poems emerged more or less chronologically. We can examine the book, therefore, to see whether the threads, which she tells us sometimes take a poet years to discern for herself, develop as the subjects, images, and themes emerge over time. No attempt has been made editorially to impose any such readings. Each reader is free to reconstruct the book, to group poems together and imagine how they might make larger, more significant patterns, or to read them as a rough chronicle of the poet's creative life in poetry in the last months of her life.

—*Paul A. Lacey*